C0-EFM-642

Happy Trails & Best Wishes!!

Sven LINDAUER

The Art and Crafts of Ancient Scandinavia
by
D. Sven Lindauer

Text by Vivian Kuala
Graphic Layout by Doug Nordberg
All Original paintings, storyline, concept
by D. Sven Lindauer
Copyright 2017-2021 Mjolnir Publishing LLC

OFFICIAL SECOND PRINTING
The Art and Crafts of Ancient Scandinavia
COPYRIGHT 2022 by Mjolnir Publishing LLC

Copyright 2017-2021 by Mjolnir Pubblishing LLC
All Rights Reserved

Mjolnir Publishing P.O. Box 2721 Cody, Wyoming 82414

Library of Congress Cataloging-in-publication Data is available upon request

No part of this book may be reproduced or transmitted in any form by any means, electronic or mechanical, including photocopying, recording, or by any other information storage and retrieval system, without written permission from the publisher.
ISBN: 978-0-578-79540-9

Printed in the United States of America

Mjolnir Publishing
Printed by Anderberg Innovative Print Solutions
6999 Oxford St. St. Louis Park, Minnesota 55426

Foreword

For more than 5 years, after reading academic papers every morning, thru hurricane, divorce, financial collapse, pandemic, and practically every obstacle a human being could endure, it was not easy staying on track, executing each painting, {even though some thought i was daft,} gathering amazing folk to model in period clothing for photoshoots for each theme, and just flatout trusting in myself and my work, to bring new light to the world about one of the most misunderstood and misrepresented cultures on the planet, my ancestors, The Norse.
This art gallery book showcases not the dark stories of the "Vikings" that were written about them centuries later after the Viking Age, which roughly began in 600 CE, lasting until the early crusades after 1000 CE.. This story i have chosen to bring is a day in the life story of folk who were originally farmers, hunters, fishermen, and skilled craftspeople who ultimately became merchants, that traveled much of the known world, eventually colonizing an area encompassing parts of North America, Iceland, Greenland, modern scandinavia today, and much of central europe all the way to Siberia, with colonies having been in Spain and north Africa as well. Now, these industrious people didnt stay every place they colonized, but trust me, according to my Academic friends, they were there, and knew early on, to create commerce for the generations, not go in to rob and burn villiages.
True, they were quite skilled in combat when called upon, but originally trained to protect family, community, and the tribes once called the Germanic people who gave the Romans a great heartache.
It is my hope that more folk become proud of thier ancestry, just as any and all ethnic groups should be, by reading the facts from archeological discoveries that today continue to destroy the dark myths, regardless of who or whom you are.
No debates are needed as much as people need to go to the root of who they are, and that comes from knowing and understanding your ancestors.
Not what someone else tells you, but what you can research and find out for yourself, in fact and proof discovered.

The Stonecutter – Gotland

Stepping back in time, between 800-900 CE, this painting takes place on the island of Gotland, off the eastern coast of Sweden. The Stonecutter's art, captured in stone, has actually given modern archaeologists a window into the culture of ancient Scandinavia.

The heroic story designed by this craftsman shows an artist, expert stonemason, visual storyteller and runemaster. Created to memorialize a brother named Hjôrulfr, meaning "sword wolf," who had fallen in battle, its images speak of victory, honor, and celebration. What do you see in the Stonecutter's art? Perhaps it brings to mind Odin and his mighty eight-legged horse Sleipnir, the valkyries of Valhalla offering hospitality after a hard-won victory, or a hero's journey to the afterlife in a spectacular longship. The stone pictured here is known as the Tjängvide Image Stone and is in the Museum of National Antiquities in Stockholm. Over 400 image stones have been discovered on Gotland, more than anywhere else in Scandinavia.

5

An early version of the longship slips out of harbor off the island of Gotland, possibly transporting one of the magnificent image stones of the Stonecutter to its new owner.

With his specific tools, some food and water close by, the Stonecutter works for long periods of time as he crafts the memorial stone.

Proving his place as man's best friend, this ancestor of the Irish Wolfhound keeps watch over the homestead while keeping the Stonecutter company as he works.

The imagination of the Stonecutter comes to life with each tap of the hammer, a masterpiece in the making. There have been at least 15 stones found in this exact style, and deviations of a later period suggest that this master had apprentices.

The Shipbuilder – Norway

The legendary ships of ancient Scandinavia were a testament to the exceptional innovation and skill of its local craftsmen.
As much art, as engineering, the iconic longships enabled traders to travel far and wide, across oceans and deep into interior river systems, to trade and barter with the local villagers.

This painting depicts a chieftain or jarl commissioning a fleet of ships for his merchants to travel, barter, and trade. As the craftsman explains to the jarl how his ships move across the water, his daughter plays nearby with her pet bear, known as a "housebear" in Old Norway. In the background, the shipbuilder's uncle hitches logs to a team of fjord horses held steady by his wife. Showing hospitality, the shipbuilder's wife brings food to share with the Jarl.
Estimated that just one ship may require up to 40,000 labor hours to build, many dedicated craftsmen and artisans were needed from 2.5 months to a full year per ship, while also working their family farms.

Near the modern day town of Andalsnes, Romsdahlsfjorden there is evidence of ancient shipbuilding sites.

9

The Shipbuilder points out the beautiful artistry of the bow work as he explains the new engineering innovations he has crafted into his ships.

Though the process looks primitive, these craftsmen were able to split logs with amazing accuracy, knowing exactly where the wood was the strongest and where each piece would work. With a shallow draft and hull that would flex, these ships were seaworthy even in the most turbulent of ocean travel.

This craft was heavy, hard work but many hands made it all come together, speeding the time to get the ships into the water and the jarl's merchants on their way to ports throughout the region.

A bear cub for a pet!
It was customary in Old Norway to bring a bear cub home to raise, as they were referred to as "Housebears" This little girl is having great fun with her playful friend.

The Sail Makers - Sweden

Sails started to be used on longships around the 8th century CE. It is estimated that it took up to 30 individuals at various stages to produce one large square sail, especially if it were for an oceangoing craft.

The women on this small farmstead in Sweden handled the full process. This began with shearing sheep since longship sails were most often made of wool. This wool came from northern European short-tailed sheep, and their unusual coat was a key element in making it work.

These sheep are double-coated, with an outside, long haired coat and a shorter, slightly softer inner coat. Using the coarse outer hairs in the sail's warp (the vertical fibers) and soft inner hairs for the weft (horizontal fibers) filled gaps in the weave. The material was then treated to shrink slightly and tighten the fabric, then coated finally by a resinous material. Leather strips of walrus hide were typically used on the sails to reinforce them and help them keep their shape when wet. They were then usually finished off with linen embroidery.

13

Every step of making this longship sail was handled by these women artisans. Depending upon the size of the ship to be fitted, it could take up to five years to make a proper sail.

Always a helpful worker on the farm, this gaited horse was an ancestor of the Norwegian Fjord horse.

This illustrates the many steps that craftswomen needed to create a sail, beginning with shearing the sheep, spinning the thread, making leather strips, weaving, cutting and sewing. And in the time it took to make a large sail, this young girl may grow up to be one of the artisans to finish it.

These women made sure that every stitch was tight and exact, as the cold wet winds of the North Sea and Atlantic Ocean were unforgiving in a storm.

The Navigator – Faroe Islands

Below the craggy west coast cliffs of Streymoy, the largest of today's Faroe Islands, this painting depicts an ancient sailor and his wife in a small clinker-built version of the longship called the "karve" as they test out the fabled "Sunstone."

Believed to be made of Icelandic spar or a similar mineral, on cloudy days this stone was used like a magnifying glass to direct and focus light from the Sun into a beam, illuminating a wooden compass floating in a bucket onboard, showing direction based on its shadow upon the wooden compass wheel. Atlantic puffins fly nearby, and seals appear interested in the process, too, coming in close to assess what is going on, whitch also was important information for the Navigator. These mariners were well-versed in reading weather patterns in the sky, watching migration and movement of birds and marine life, and could tell whether they were near land or crossing the open ocean just from a taste of the water.

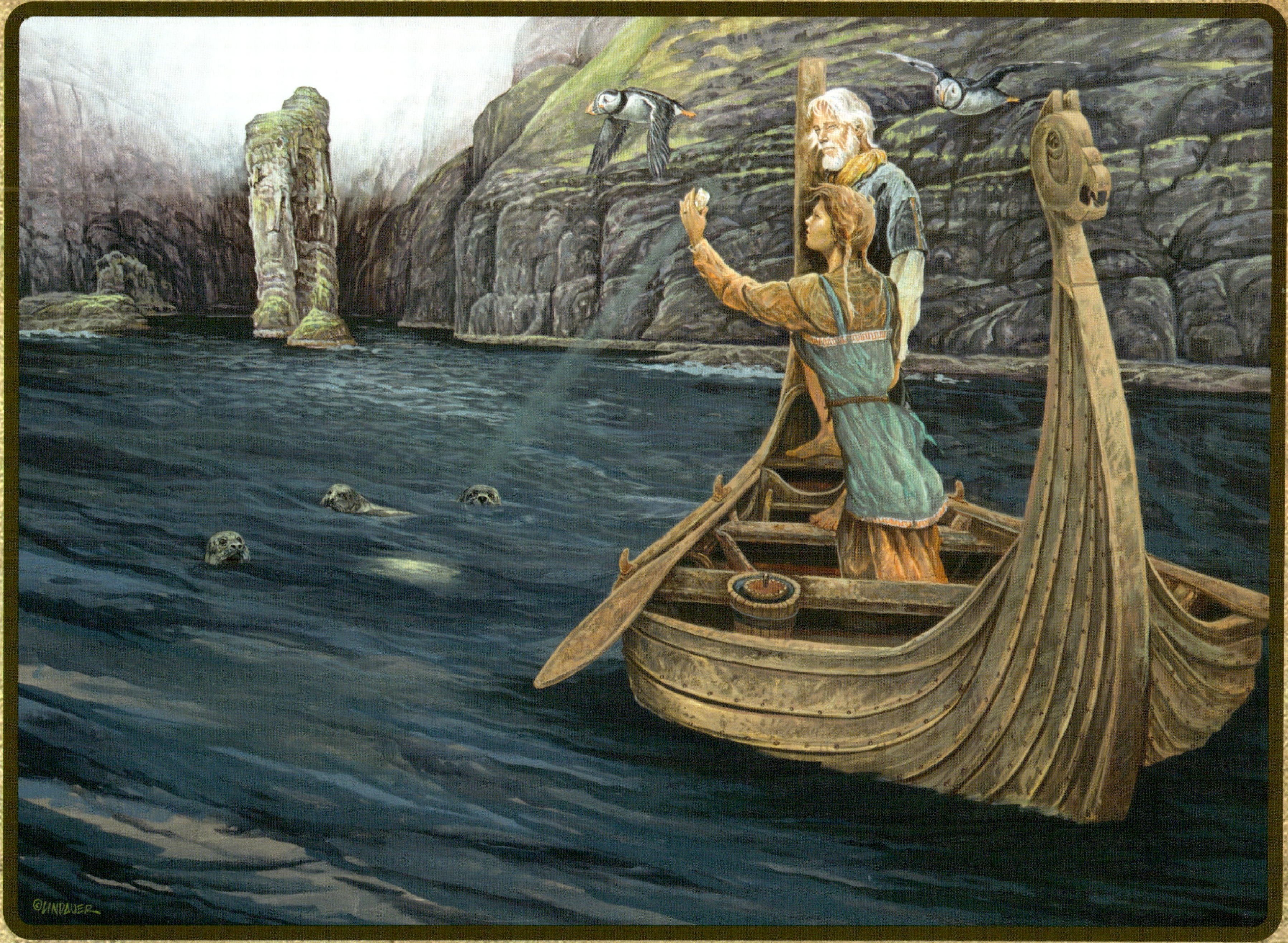
©LINDAUER

The navigator is testing one of the most important instruments to be developed for travel by sea — a floating compass called a "solskuggefjøl" helping them determine direction when there was no land in sight to use for reference.

The beautiful, craggy cliffs of Stremoy were one of many amazing environs that the Norse colonized and thrived in, and to this day hold signs of the Old Ways.

Another amazing innovation reported to have been used for open-sea travel by Norse sailors was the sunstone. When clouds obscured the sun enough that they could not tell where it was in the sky, the sunstone concentrated the light to illuminate the compass.

North Atlantic seals curiously found the sunstone's beam of light and came to investigate.

The Skald Poet – Denmark

The art of spoken words, the turn of a phrase, the surprise twist – such was the craft of the Skald.

Skalds helped preserve Scandinavia's largely oral history, mythologies, and laws, by learning and sharing them in public. The meters and forms of the skald's poetry took advantage of wordplays such as kennings that describe a person or event rather than give its name. It was a game to try and find the most unique way to describe a very familiar character or story without actually saying who or what it was. Audiences loved it.

They would learn from the skalds and then pass them along, being perfect entertainment for long winter nights. In this painting a skald is practicing her craft and honing her skills to get ready to perform at court or the Althing.

She has collected a discerning group of small admirers in the Danish forest, where she weaves her cryptic and captivating artform. Skaldic poetry, originally carved in runic inscriptions, later became some of the first examples of writing on paper. Among the most famous examples we have today are the Hávamál, The Poetic Edda and Snorri Sturluson's The Prose Edda.

21

An excellent example of the beautiful workmanship of women's clothing, with lovely decorations and jeweled pieces used for fasteners.

This fox and cottontail rabbit have been captivated, it seems, by the Skald. That speakswell for her performance!

A beautiful bird known as the Common Rosefinch has landed nearby and listens attentively to the Skald as she weaves her tale.

A European deer and European brown hare are in awe of the enchanting stories spun by this talented Skald.

The Village Builders – Scotland

Taking place in Northern Scotland around 780 C.E.
this painting depicts the beginning of a colony among the standing
stones on Alltan Dubh, also known as Laide of Reiff.
The Norse settled here as well as other parts of Scotland
and Ireland. It was customary to build structures near
signs of earlier dwellings, such as the standing stones.
There is evidence of this at Jarlshof ruins in Shetland of
Iron Age structures known to be of Nordic origin.
In this painting, you see both men and women involved in
building the longhouse which eventually served as the
communal center of the village.
One individual is carving beams with an axe,
while a craftsman on the roof structure straightens posts
from above, and stonemasons below build exterior walls, with
a clay oven burning for firing various objects used in the
construction, and a display of tools on a worktable nearby.
A Norwegian Lundhund runs amidst the construction
as ancestors of todays Icelandic cattle graze in the background....

25

Villagers work together to get the longhouse ready for winter. Every craftsperson has a specific skillset that they employed during construction.

Perhaps construction was not her primary job in the village, but when necessary everyone pitched in to do whatever they could. The norse were hard working, and this ethic served them well as they ventured out to find new lands.

Norse architecture was both beautiful and functional, with touches of innovation that were signature to Scandinavians. Everything was built or produced on site, including clay pieces fired in this outdoor oven.

Skill, imagination and the right tools were integral to a well-built structure, intended to brave the weather and keep inhabitants warm and secure.

The Musicians – Finland

Music! It is an art and its instruments are beautiful crafts that seem to appeal to everyone, ancient and modern, in magical ways.

In this painting, one can almost hear the singing and laughter as this gifted family of musicians enjoys playing music together in the muted acoustics of the forest in what is now Finland.
The drum beat rumbles deeply as though coming from the heart of the earth and the horn calls out boldly to the wind, accompanied by the gentle tones of a stringed harp.
As the jouhikko is gently played she sings a song of her ancestors. This musical family has also attracted some wild visitors listening to the music, tails wagging. A roe deer and finnish tree squirrel join the family's "Finnish Spitz", an early dog breed.
Remnants of these ancient instruments have been discovered in Finland and Karelia, including the tuning keys.
Very few actual musical compositions from this time period exist today. Amazingly, though, modern archaeomusicologists are working on resurrecting the tunes using notes available from the reconstruction of ancient instruments! We may hear again the forgotten songs of these ancient lands.

29

Music has a way of spreading pure joy. Having family to share music with multiplies that joy. Their faces say it all.

Even the most timid of creatures responds to the beauty of music. This long eared member of the squirrel family doesn't want to miss out!

The Finnish forest resounds with the beat of a beautiful drum, the pulse of the music that finds its way to the soul. Acadamiens have wirtten papers on the drum in northern europe being seen more in some areas than others.. Finland being one of them.

This roe deer and dog might usually be wary of each other in nature, but in the presence of this haunting music, they share peace.

The Herbalist - Iceland

In a hidden cave beneath the breathtaking northern lights
of the Icelandic aurora borealis, this woman has sprinkled
dried flowers into the fire to illuminate her work.
This helped focus thoughts and prayers for her village.
She drew a rune, one of the letters of the Old Norse futhark,
or language, knowing immediately that it was very good.
It was Jera, the symbol of a good year and abundant harvest.

The Herbalist felt centered, grounded in the Earth. She understood
the weather and read the signs left by Nature. She could feel
the elements and knew the art of working with them in humility.
Clad in a sealskin received as a gift from her mother, she held
out an iron rod with gem and sent the blessings on their way.
Holding the Jera rune in her hand, she raised up, giving thanks.

Gazing upon the aurora again. She relaxed into the beauty.
Nature is so wondrously bountiful, she thought.
Soon to start planting with everyone this new moon, for now
she could just be still and know that all was well.

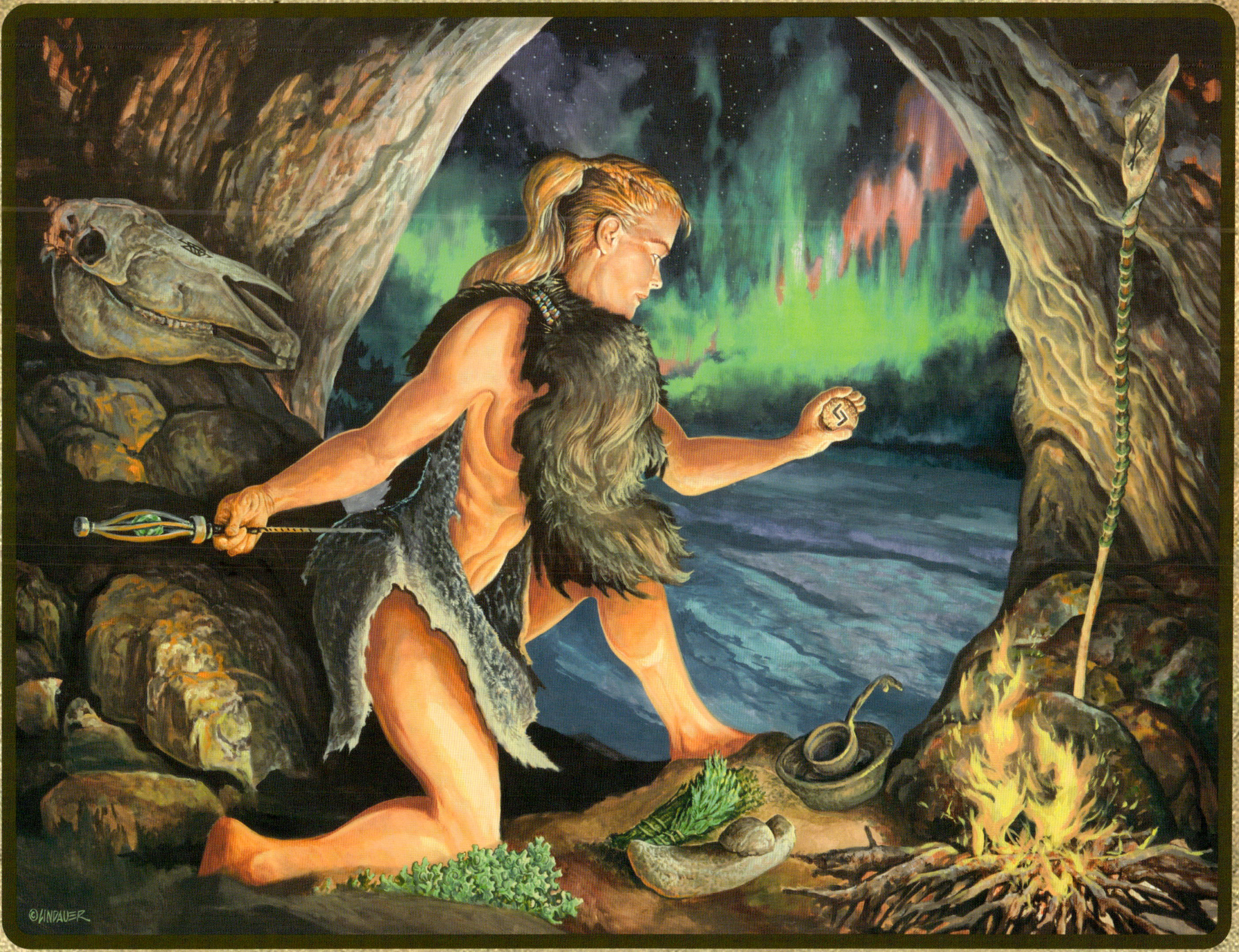

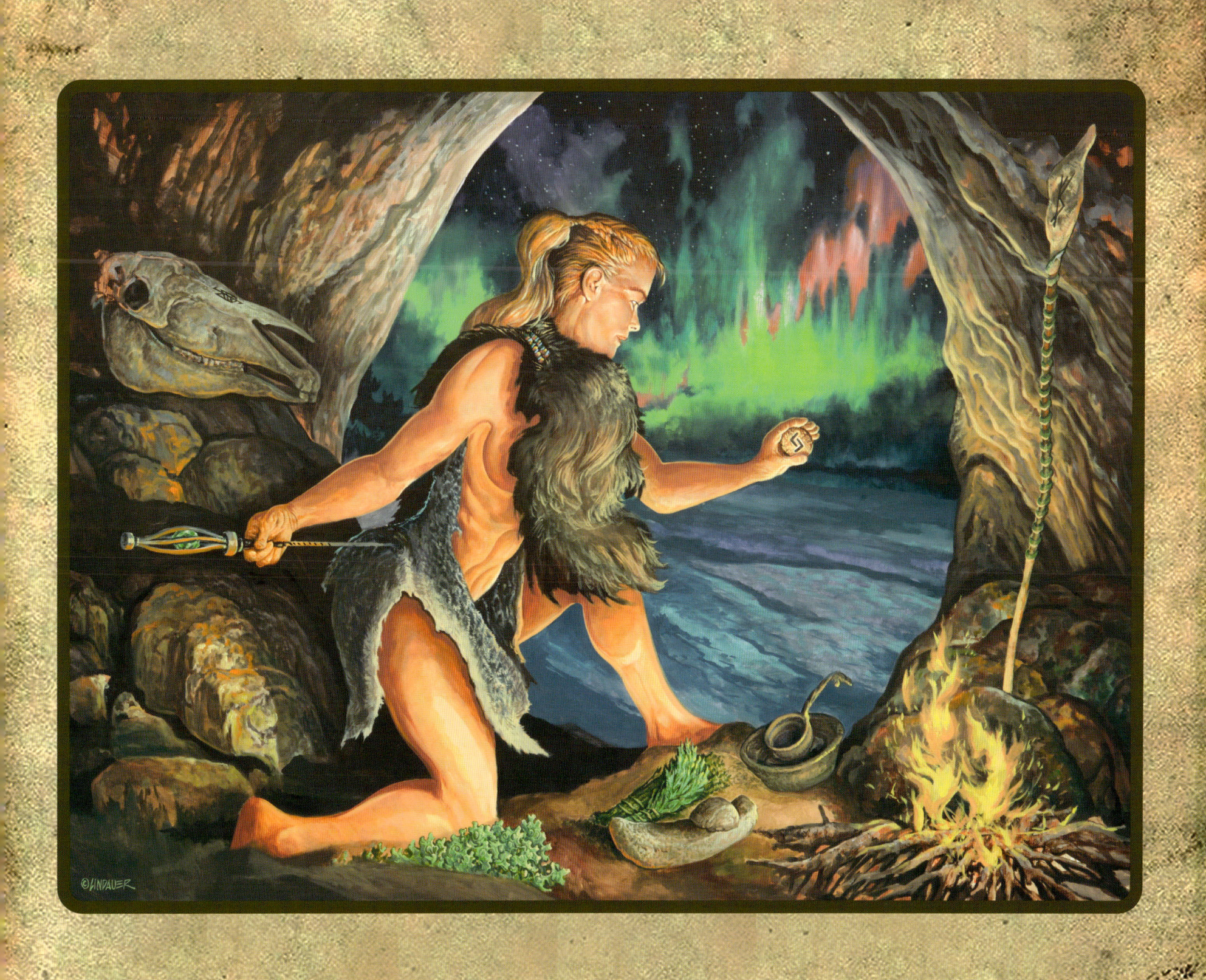

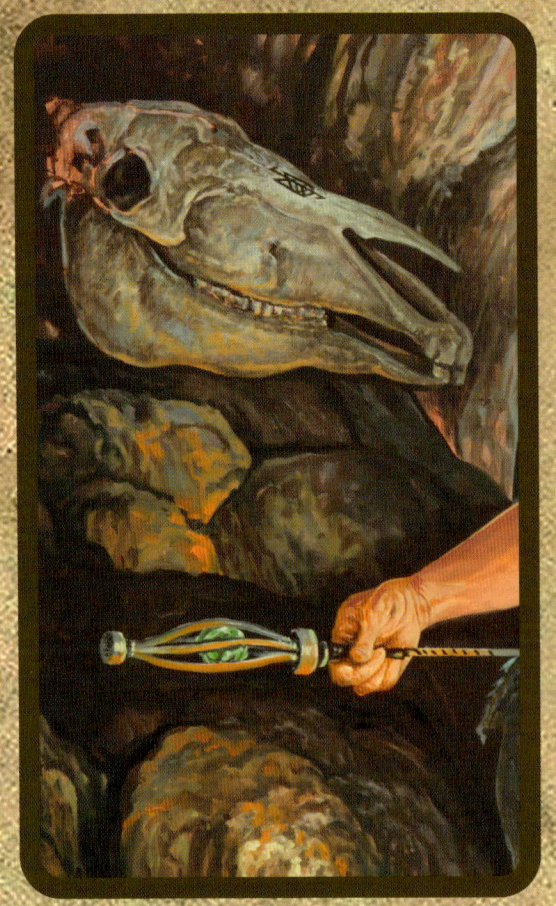

The Herbalist holds in her hand a beautiful wand made of iron. At its top is a setting holding a magnificent stone found in the volcanic lands of Iceland, a symbol of the energies of life.

The Herbalist lived simply. Much-used quern-stones were always close by. Including the bottom stationary quern and the upper muller or handstone used for hand grinding her herbs and grains.

A powerful and stunning sight, the aurora borealis lit up the sky with its glorious colors and subtle energies. A perfect time for the Herbalist to make plans and set her intentions of a good year for the village.

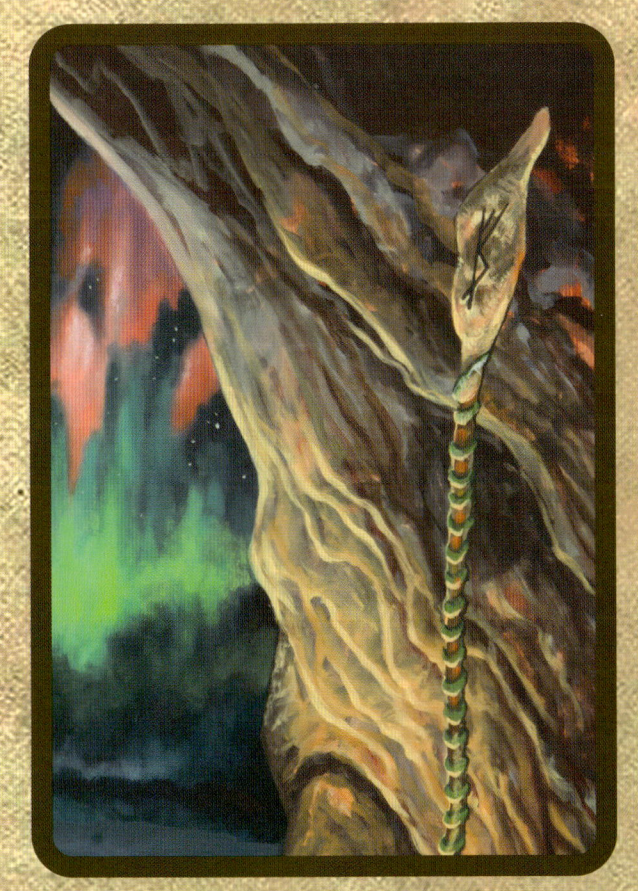

The wooden staff was a symbol that everyone recognized. Villagers knew they could come to her for help and counsel. Much revered and appreciated, the Herbalist's art flowed as wisdom and skill.

The Blacksmith - Denmark

The loud clanging of hammer on anvil and hiss of the charcoal were proof that a blacksmith's forge was nearby.
In any village throughout ancient Scandinavia, the busy smithy was a hub of activity, because the blacksmith was a craftsman whose abilities were needed by almost everyone. For local customers, who were mostly farmers, builders,and protectors of their homesteads, the blacksmith forged farm tools, metal door lock mechanisms, pike and spear tips, horseshoes, chain, swords, cooking utensils and much more. For other craftsmen of the village such as stonemasons, woodcarvers and shipbuilders, the blacksmith created specialized tools of their trades, as well.
While utility and efficiency were key, the blacksmith also had an eye for artistry and beauty.
In this painting, the heavy blows of this Hedeby smithy pound out a familiar staccato as he forges his latest work. A Norwegian Forest cat, whose domestic ancestors arrived centuries earlier by ship, carries out his duty as chief mouser of the forge, while a young Manx Loughtan goat wanders among the spark, shadow and lightplay of the anvil and bellows.

37

The Blacksmith forge was the hub of the village. Everyone needed his services at one time or another, from castle to homestead, craftsmen and artisans. Goats were in multitude among these settlements, providing milk, and other special attributes used in old norse society.

A few of the blacksmith's wares are depicted here including all types of knives, small hand tools, an axe and seax. A warrior's helmet would have been a special order that needed to be fitted perfectly. Alongside the tools is a close-up of the double bellows this blacksmith used.

The process of making an exceptional sword was grueling. For the finest workmanship it often required an apprentice to constantly work the bar with heavy hammers, layer upon layer of the finest metals.

This mouser and companion always seemed to know the best place to settle down for surveilance. This particular breed of feline traveled on ships headed to settlement throughout the Viking age.

39

The Bowyer – Norway

Using the finest Norwegian woods from forests along the fjords, this painting represents a skilled craftsman, and artisan who specialized in creating bows and arrows for daily use or specialty purpose, such as hunting equipment and necessary weapons, to protect family and home.

Bowyers developed several styles of bows, making adjustments for how each one would be used and often giving them a distinctive signature look for their more affluent clients. The longbow, principally used for long range shooting, and the medium length hunting bow, best used on foot. A special horsebow was also designed, proportioned for use while horseback. Centuries later these designs are still in use.

Quality arrows were just as important as a masterfully crafted bow. The arrow shafts depicted here were made from small branches or saplings, then finally worked into shape by running them through and across carved stone channels to keep them straight and accurate.

The Bowyer's wife, a marksman in her own right, tests and target shoots a horsebow to determine its handling and accuracy.

41

The Bowyer bends and shapes his creations into powerful tools. Situated along the verdant coast of one of Norway's spectacular fjords, he had a resource-filled environment to make quality bows and arrows.

Scandinavian women were often skilled in the use of the bow. Here, the Bowyer's wife puts his creations to the test. Only the best will do.

Ah, the family cat. *W*ith no mousing to do, she finds a nice warm lap to curl up in and allow the day go by. *A* quiver of arrows is slung over the arm of the *B*owyer's chair, each matched feather and precision shaft attesting to his expertise.

*C*hanneled stones were precisely carved to train the wood for the *B*owyer's arrow shafts to be straight and true. *T*hat made accurate arrows.

The Culinary Arts - Denmark

In many Norse communities, food preparation was a family or village affair. Even with its harsh winters, Scandinavia is recognized as having one of the healthiest diets on the planet. When making sure that everyone had food appropriate to their needs, the Norse had it down to an art.

There was definitely an art to gathering healthy food from the forest, lake, garden or wild environs, to the family table, with as much artistry in the coordination as the cooking. The Norse excelled at animal husbandry, gardening, hunting, fishing and wildcrafting. Add to that their knowledge of long-term storage, drying, fermentation, building root cellars and other types of food preservation. It was to be diligent and work together. Special songs were sung to help mark cooking intervals. Grandmother's recipes along with her "secret ingredients" became the comfort food of the next generations. This multi-generational time of participation and gathering served them well, and ultimately taught the cornerstone of the Norse tradition: Hospitality!

45

The preparation of food for a family or a village was an important art. When survival depended upon your work and meticulous preparation throughout the year, every part of the process was watched over with care and diligence.

Summertime was perfect for outdoor cooking and welcoming guests. With everyone pitching in and sharing, a wonderful feast could be had by all. Of course, the community goat is hoping someone will slip up and drop a morsel or two.

Fowl in ancient Scandinavia were not exceptionally big, but they were hardy and produced many eggs. Key to the culinary arts was knowing how to dry, pickle, smoke or salt meat and eggs for use over the winter. Holes were dug in the ground to preserve meats, as well.

One of the most important jobs of any home was tending the fire. Oftentimes it was the job of one person to continuously monitor the fire so it would never go out, but also conserve fuel, regulate the temperature and safety. Sitting around a fire can be a bonding experience, a time for eating, sharing, storytelling, and gazing in silence — a great place for inspiration and renewal.

The Jeweler – Ireland

In the Norse colony of Dubh-Lynn which would later become Dublin, Ireland, a young woman creates beautiful, wearable art. Her jewelry, artfully designed and crafted, became very popular so she spends her time making commissioned items to meet the significant trade demands. This craftsperson uses a small clay oven to produce molten metal that she pours into handmade clay molds. The most popular pieces then were Apron Brooches. Norse jewelry found in archeological digs worldwide were incredibly intricate and complex. Also crafting metal keys and other small cast objects such as hammers of Thor and pendants depicting Freyja, her daughter's favorite so, she made a special necklace for her, the real jewel in her life. In awe, the jeweler's young daughter holds up into the streaming sunlight a necklace made of pure Amber, another much-admired gemstone, the traders promoted for her. Even the pet ferret seems to be fascinated by the play of light through these translucent gemstones.

49

With careful attention to detail, the Jeweler crafts many sought after pieces to be marketed far and wide by the village merchants.

Its a good possibility that this young girl will apprentice with her mother to become a master of this craft and hand it down through generations.

A display of the Jeweler's valuable molds and small cast pieces, including the lovely Freyja necklace. Trade beads used came from many different parts of the world.

This curious pet ferret is both friend and helper in the Jeweler's household. Many wild animals were found and brought home to be pets in ancient Norse culture.

The Woodcarver – Sweden

One of the earliest styles of ornamental art in ancient Scandinavia was woodcarving. This painting depicts one of the many artisans who could turn beauty into function. A woodcarver had to master the whole process, not just one or two steps. He had to learn the characteristics of all kinds of trees and have the understanding, strength and skill to harvest, prepare and craft each piece. It paid to start learning early, and the best way to learn was as an apprentice.

A young person who displayed an aptitude for a specific skillset was encouraged to work with a master craftsman and learn every aspect of the art from an early age. Once skilled, he would probably carve the bow or starboard parts of a sailing vessel or design and create columns and doors for lodges.
.The craftsman in this painting seems quite young, but he has spent many years learning his craft. Now he confidently works on his own projects. Proud of his owner in his own special way, the pet fox celebrates him by bringing a present – in the form of a mouse.

53

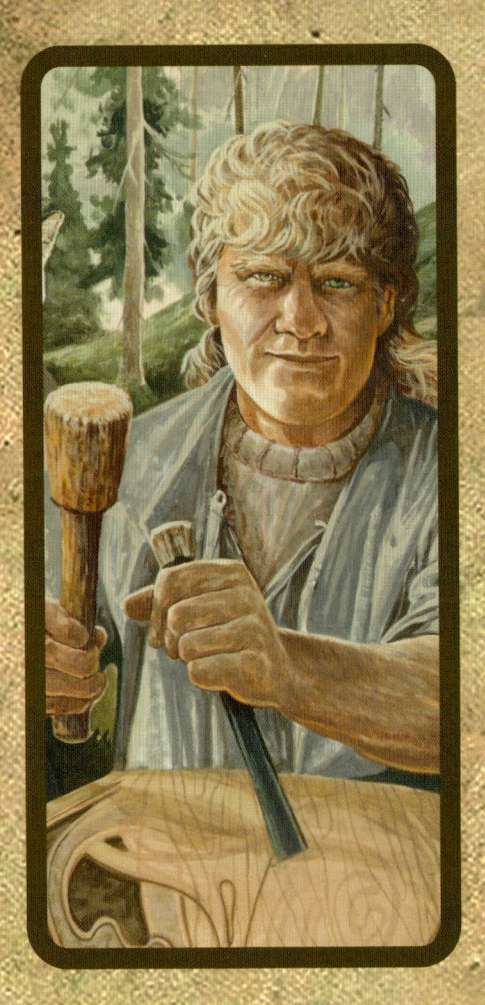

From apprentice to master craftsman and artisan in his own right, now the Woodcarver can take his skill and make the art his own.

The European Red Fox ranged throughout northern and central Europe, much like the species known today in the US.

With imagination and skill, these simple tools created a masterpiece like the dragon's head, designated for a mighty longship.
An assortment of very sharp chisels with a drillbit were crafted for the carver by an incredibly skilled blacksmith using steel that would hold an edge while working with all the hardwoods being carved.

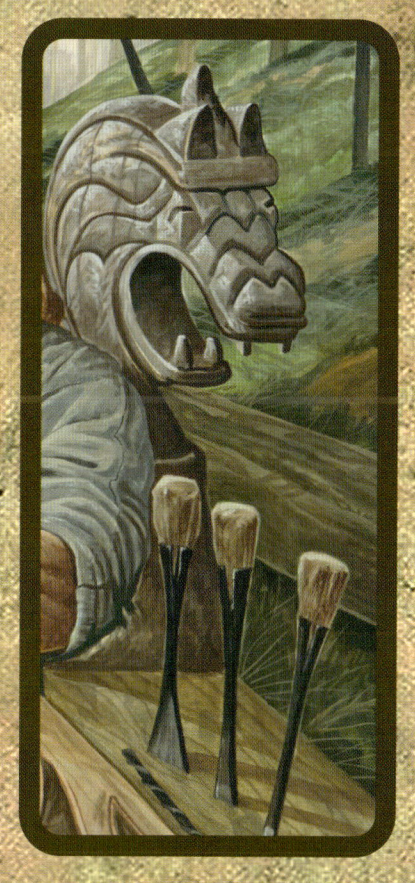

Popular during the early Viking era was the Broa design. The first to depict a flowing and intertwining subject, it often showcased Jörmungandr, the world serpent, or the great wolf Fenrir from Norse lore.

The Healer – Netherlands

It was a dark day when this man found his calling. One of a dozen warriors chosen by their king in the heat of battle, he was ordered to stop fighting and start binding up as many wounded as he could. Women healers who traveled with the army had more than they could handle. So these young men quickly went to work alongside the women, following their lead, and learning new skills with every warrior they tried to treat. Once battle finally ended, the king allowed them to continue to work with the healers throughout the campaign, acquiring reputation in the medical arts. Once home, this man decided to become an apprentice. He grew in skill as he learned to treat both injuries and illness, as well as how to find, prepare and administer the classical herbal remedies until soon, he struck out on his own. Acting as doctor, dentist or veterinarian, the young Healer traveled from village to village. It was a momentous occasion when the Healer arrived. Several notable families of physicians descended from that intrepid group of young healers.

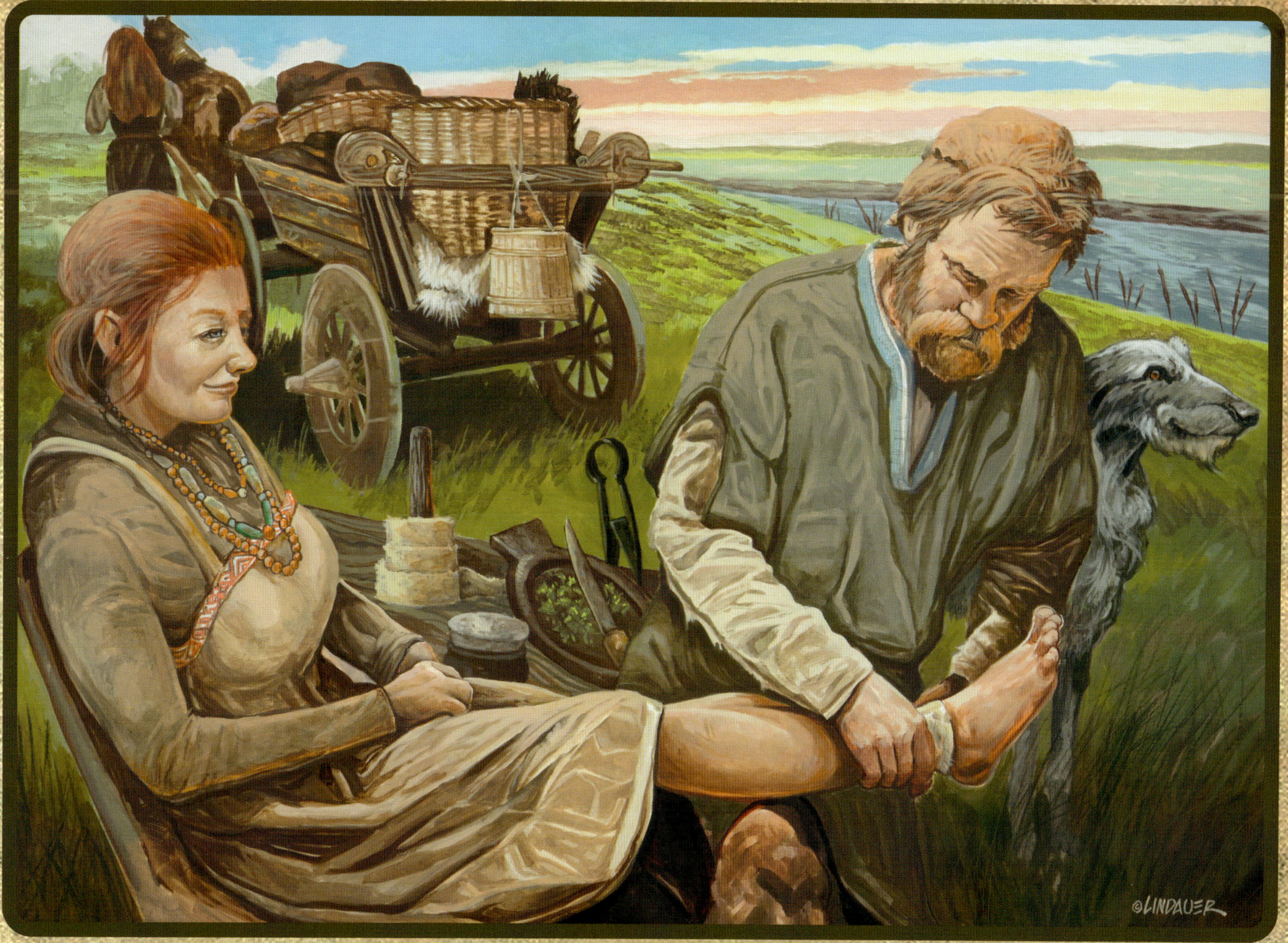
©LINDAUER

Thankful for the help of an experienced Healer, a village woman looks forward to getting her ankle treated.

The Healer's happy companion and friend is an elegant Sighthound who lends his own quiet confidence to the skilled Healer.

The traveling Healer's cart made even this wide expanse of Dutch outdoors a welcome place for a house call.

A gentle touch and skilled hands made short work to stabilize this injury and put it on the road to complete healing.

The Horsetrainers - Iceland

For many ceturies Horses have played an important part in Norse culture, as a skilled horsetrainer knew how to harness their power and mobility.

This painting depicts activities involved in training these horses. A craft that goes back thru millennia was initiated to create a good relationship between horse and rider. A man and wife team are working a young horse to prepare it to be ridden as a saddle horse or pull a wagon or sled, if necessary.

A descendant of the Norwegian Fjord horse, the beautiful Icelandic horses pictured here are sturdy and "gaited," meaning a horse moves in such a way that its movement will be smooth and comfortable to the rider.

The groundwork begins in the roundpen.

The man in foreground is preparing to hobble this young horse, so it will have the freedom to graze but not wander off into the open range. It also created patience and discipline, reducing panic and flightiness.

As training goes on, the horse will be introduced to the bridle and bit, the saddle and, in winter, snowshoes, shown hanging on the fence.

61

Beautiful Icelandic horses are much valued in the horse world. They are long-lived and hardy, and the breed is still used for traditional sheepherding, as well as leisure, showing and racing!

Despite their smaller stature Icelandic horses are strong and known for their spirited temperament and large personality.

Keeping it in the family, this little rascal with her own toy horse is watching, learning, and will someday grow up to be a master horse trainer in her own right.

With proper training, young horses accept the bit, bridle, and saddle along with their riders. From various archeologigical finds, this horse equipment remains unchanged in design many centuries later.

The Potter – Poland

Of recent interest to archaeologists tracing the historic movement of the Norse settlements, are two areas that are today the Republic of Poland. In the Viking era it is believed they were important places of Scandinavian settlement. Including a large colony and trading center, several buildings housing a wide range of craft activities and residences for up to 70 men and women, these areas were also home to beautiful crafts including pottery.

A combination of art and craft, pottery served important daily functions in ancient Scandinavia. For instance, storage of food and beverages in the cold northern climates required durable containers easy to seal tight. Wooden vessels were less so. From this trading center, many folk were able to get high quality pottery for this use.

In this painting a craftsman is shaping clay pottery on a foot and rope-driven pottery wheel. The clay soil in this and surrounding areas made it a good choice to work as a potter. Archaeologists today are able to trace the origins of pottery shards found by studying the specific clay content.

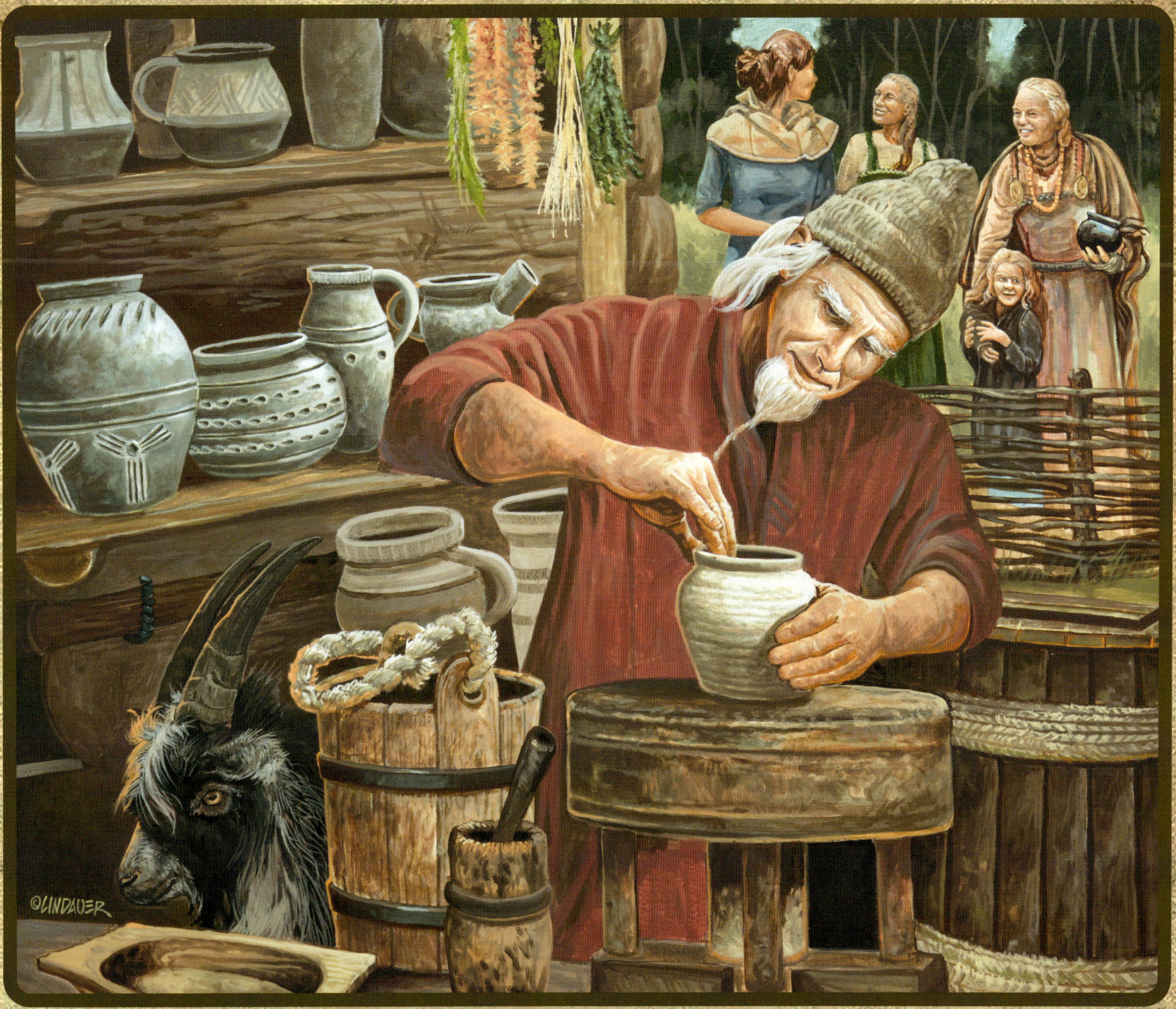
©LINDAUER

This "high tech" potter's wheel of its day enabled potters to make very high quality pieces much faster than if he had to produce them by shaping each one individually on a stationary slab.

The potter's wheel also allowed for much variety in crafting the shape. Once completed the pottery was artistically decorated, making it both useful and beautiful.

This Finnish Landrace goat, an ancient breed still in existence today, is keeping a close watch on the potter's shop. Who knows when something good to eat might show up in one of those beautiful containers!

Women from the village compare their new pottery purchases and make plans for buying more before winter sets in.

The Mead Maker - Jorvik

The Norse colony of Jorvik was a place of commerce and travel in the early Viking Age. Mead was not only an important trade good, but an important element of daily life when available.

The craftsperson creating this unperishable alcoholic beverage was both chemist and artist. The basic ingredients needed to make this early recipe of mead were simply honey and water, but if they were combined and fermented improperly it was not drinkable. A skilled mead maker knew how to use the right amount of ingredients and let it ferment under the right conditions to craft an amazing drink that would not perish in heat or cold. In this painting, the beautiful location of this pub is the perfect atmosphere for enjoying time with friends. Testing this new batch of mead, a few of his patrons seem very well pleased with the outcome.

Daughter of the Meadmaker shows her fascination with the creators of Honey by decorating the traveling cart of Mead vessels.

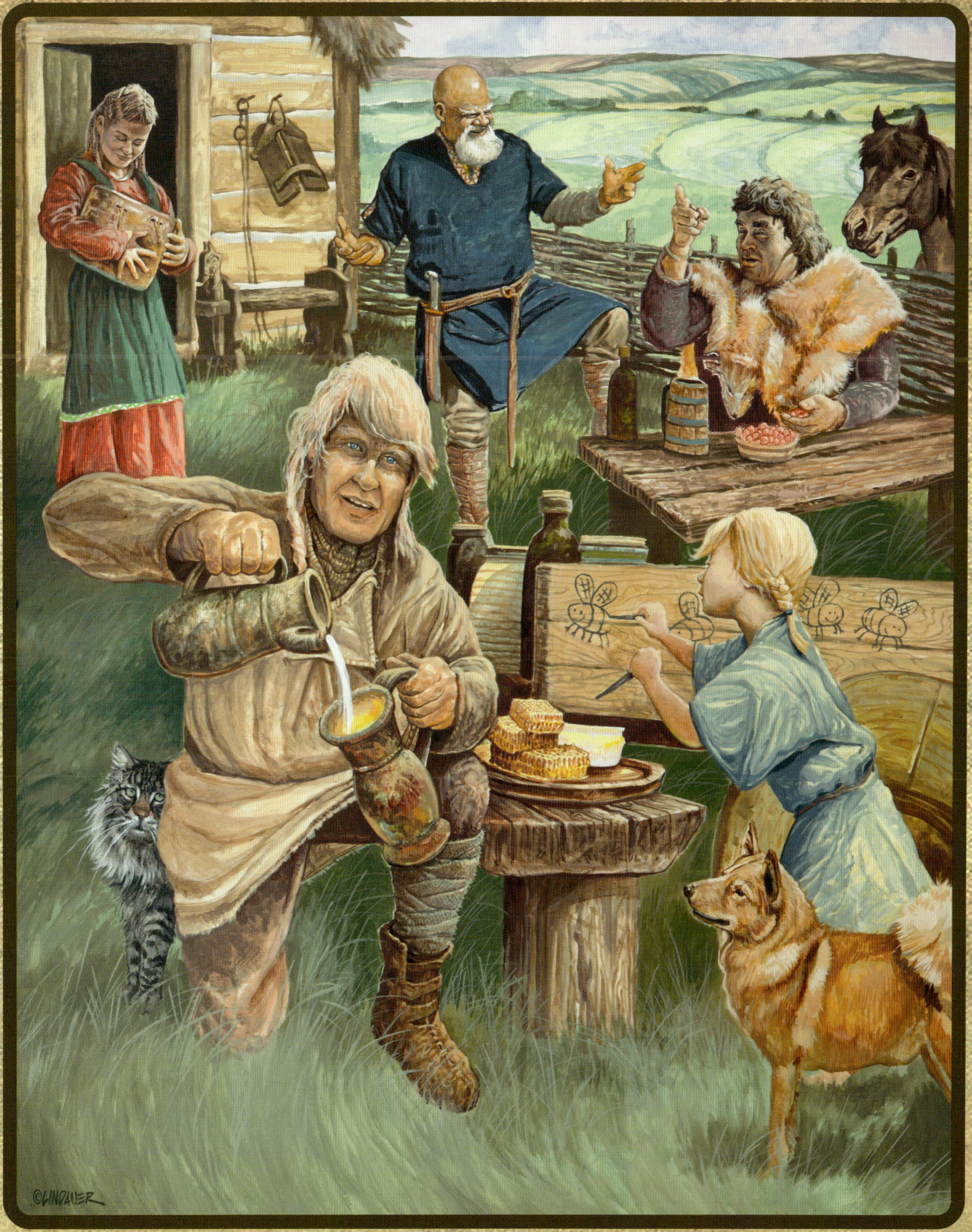
©LINDAUER

There is archeological evidence dating back thousands of years that mead and ale had been crafted and used as daily beverages. This craftsman pours some of his excellent brew for patrons to "test" for him.

According to myth, mead brings out the poet in those who drink it. It looks like there are some great stories being told around this fine brew.

Found in some early recipes based on availably in the region, a bucket of berries was a sweet compliment to the brewer's mead.

Bees everywhere! This budding young artist was getting in good practice, while her Finnish Spitz dog, which are known to love children, keeps watch close by.

The Merchant – Norway

During times of trade and barter, the Merchant was an integral part of commerce during the Viking Age. An art in and of itself, the methods used by a merchant to establish trade relations took a mix of diplomacy, negotiating skills and some enticing incentives to clinch a trade deal. Creating and maintaining friendships and camaraderie in villages, communities, and other countries took precedence. In this painting a man and his associates bring gifts of rare animals to a Norse chieftain and his wife.
The merchant's wife offers a beautiful polar bear hide to the chieftain as her husand and old friend of the royal couple gifts the queen a mating pair of Mongolian antelope known today as "saigas". A young muskoxen on a leash, rounds out the greeting gifts.
The Merchant and his wife have become good friends with this chieftain and Queen after many years of profitable trade. It is their hope that this friendship will last down through the generations as their children take their places in society and continue the relationship for the good of each family and their communities.

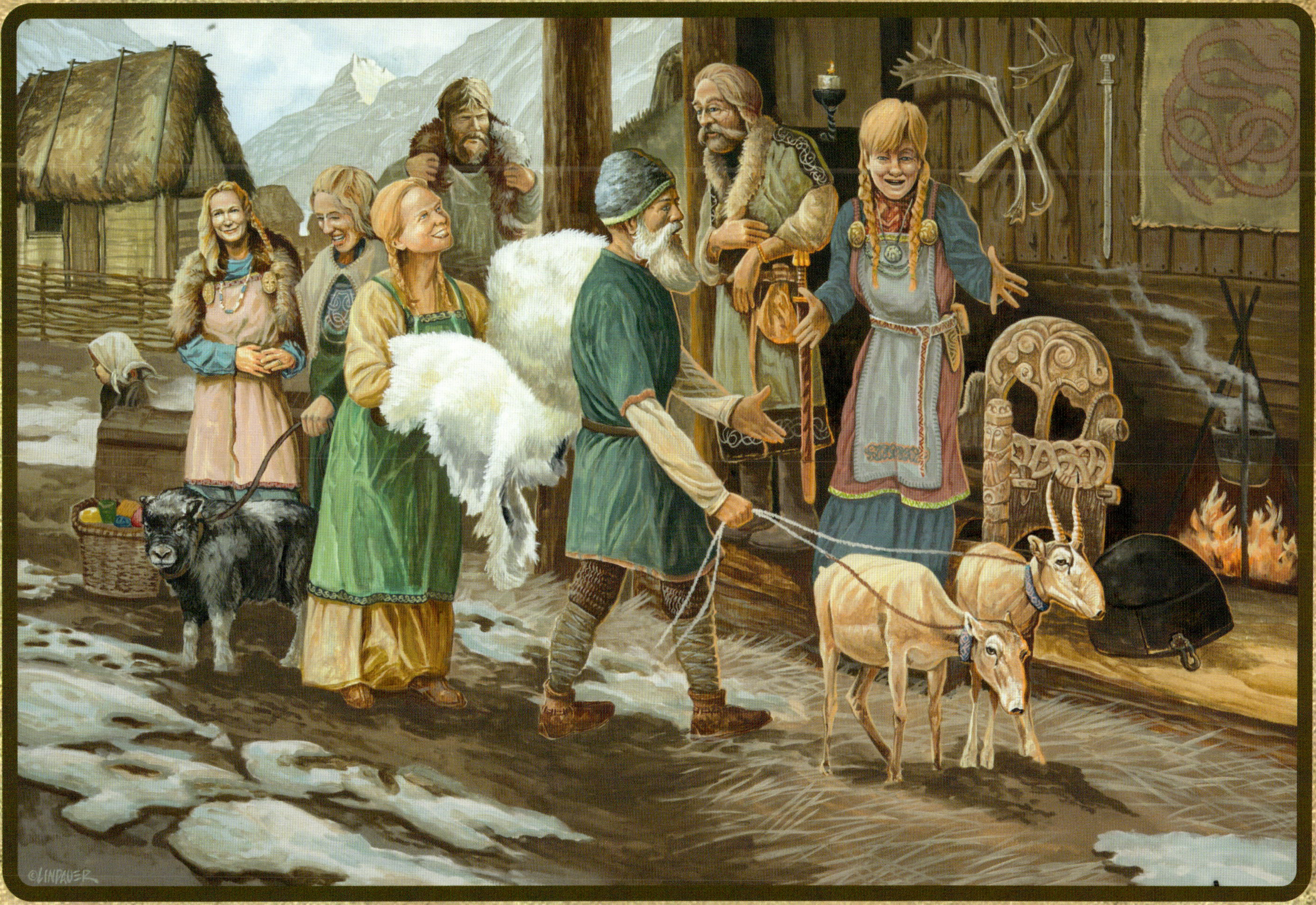
©LINDAUER

The chieftain receives a beautiful animal hide as a gift. In the cold Arctic climate, these were valuable gifts and much appreciated.

The merchant and associates brought a male muskoxen with them as a gift for the royal couple. This animal is seems manageable now, but he will be formidable when fullgrown. A few of the trade goods presented will consist of many items, including silver ingots, rare textiles such as silk, and handblown glassware from other parts of the world.

Always important in building rapport with other kingdoms, the chieftain's wife is a key resource to her husband, and responsible for offering hospitality to honored guests. Her look of sheer delight bodes well for their continued good relations.

An ancient breed of antelope, these animals still exist today but are dwindling in numbers. A mating pair would not only have been difficult to find, but to take care of and feed well during the long journey.

The Tabletweaver – Scotland

Tablet weaving is an ancient artform that became widely popular in Scandinavia during the first millennium CE. A method of using square tablets or cards with holes in them to weave narrow decorative bands made of wool, silk or linen. The threads were often tied to a post or small loom. While moving a tool back and forth through the threads, and turning the tablets made distinctive patterns appear. These norse tablet weavers were well known for their amazing skill, sometimes using threads of spun silver or gold to fashion distinctively regal patterns. Pieces of cloth bands, with the tablets themselves, were found among the treasures of the famous Oseberg ship, some loose, some attached to fine clothing. This highlighted the honor given to both the textiles and the skilled craftswomen who created them. In this painting a mother/daughter duo working on a new pattern together, made from finely spun sheep's wool collected from their prized animals. Near them a variety of woven bands are ready for barter or trade.

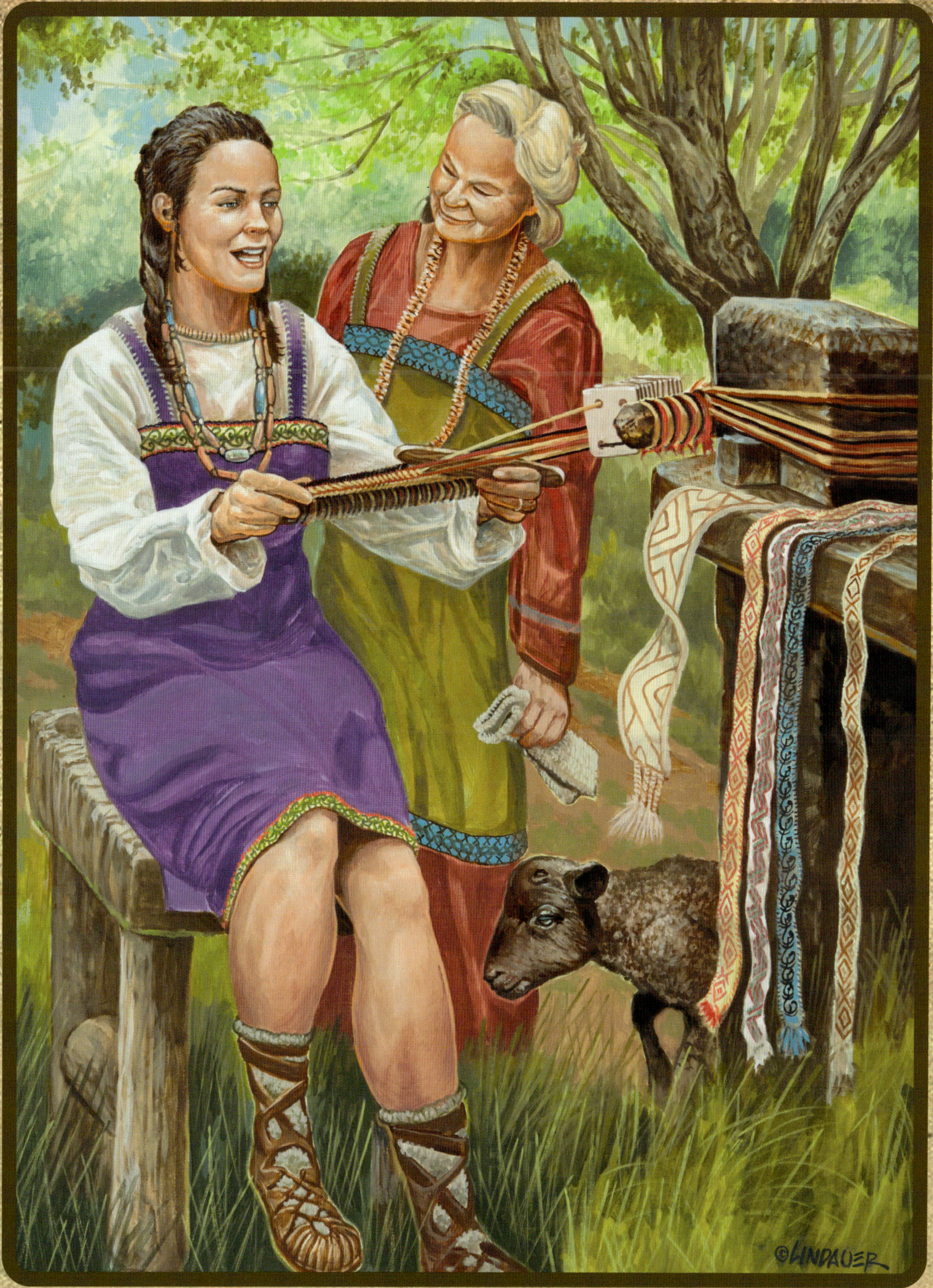
©LINDAUER

This craftsperson apprenticed with her mother, working together to create distinctive designs that would catch the eye of traders and their discerning customers throughout the world. Using the finest materials, often made themselves, they were assured of an elegant product.

The creative turning of the tablets which are strung with multiple colors of finely spun thread is key to the tabletweaver's unique designs.

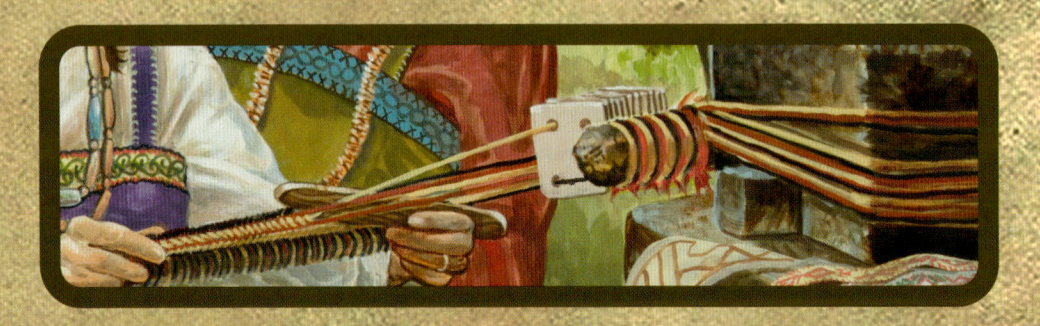

This small critter seems to know her quality wool is important to the success of this mother/daughter team.

Specific woven patterns in textiles from archeological finds define the various time periods when these unique creations were made. Digs such as Birka, Hedeby, Nydham Mose, Oseberg ship, Jutland, Skjoldenham, etc. yielded many surving items relating to ancient norse art and crafts.

Saami Drum Maker - Russia

Inhabiting Sápmi, which today encompasses parts of northern Sweden, Norway, Finland and the Kola Peninsula of northern Russia, the Saami people have herded the reindeer for thousands of years. Long before there were borders and countries with those names, these aboriginal tribes survived under some of the harshest weather conditions on earth, flourished, and were held in honor and awe by their neighbors. Also known as "laplanders", they traded prized walrus tusks, fine furs, whale oil and hunting falcons for metal products. Many Saami were farmers, laborers and fishermen, but are mostly legendary for living their lives to the cycle of the magnificent herds of reindeer.

In this painting, an elder tribe member and craftsman who creates musical instruments from reindeer hide and wood, some for entertainment, some strictly for sacred use. Under the night sky, the aurora borealis illuminates the Drum Maker's daughter chanting her "joik" to the soulful rhythm of a drum made especially for her and her song by her father. Decendants of these tribes live on today.

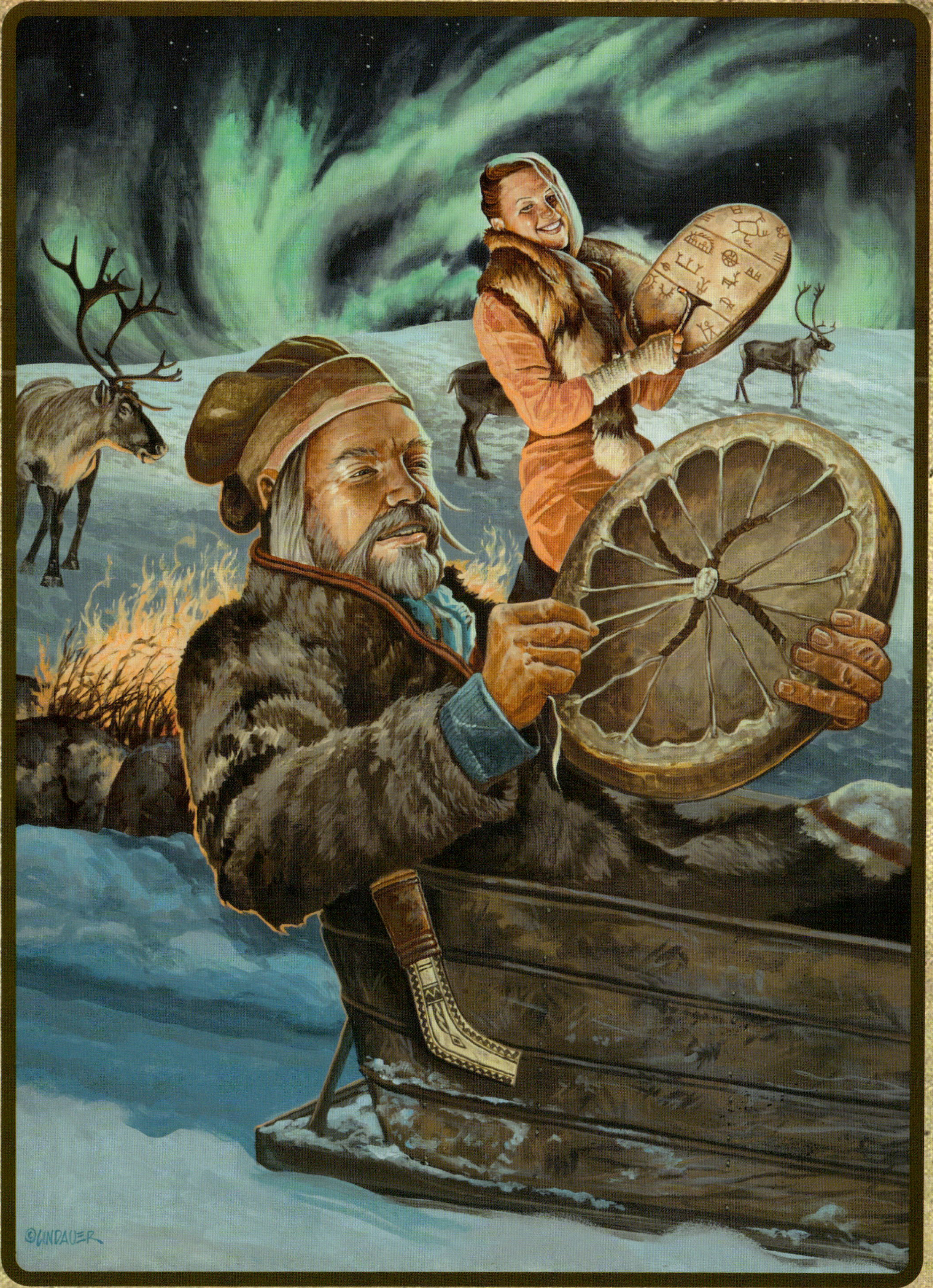

The Drum Maker's daughter delights in the artistry and magical sounds of the sacred drum gifted by her father, as the colorful "breath of the warriors" enlivens the night sky.

The cycle of the reindeer herds defines the life of Saami herdsmen. Protecting the reindeer is protecting their families, as so many of their needs are met by the abundance provided by the reindeer.

The Drum Maker sits in his pulka, a type of sled without runners, working on a new drum. His experienced and gifted hands wrap laces on the back of a drum which holds the reindeer hide in place and creates a handle to hold the drum while playing.

Always kept close by is the distinctive Saami knife, housed within a carved antler sheath decorated in a beautiful geometric tribal pattern.

Glima - Norway

Glima is the Norse form of martial arts developed by the Vikings, and is still practiced today. The word "Viking" conveys an image of resilient men and women of honor who were strong, intelligent, self-reliant, and tenacious. Glima embodies these values and teaches the fitness, strategies and focus needed for combat and self-defense. During ancient times, Norse children – both boys and girls – started training at a very early age. Glima taught them to be strong while teaching them respect and restraint. Family members had to work together, played games requiring strength and strategic thinking. They learned to hunt, fish and forage, and survive the harshness of winter. Life was unpredictable, so everyone became skilled and capable of protecting home, family, and the community.

The system of Glima includes strength-training and strategies, both for offense and defense, training a person to get fit, strong, and fight with lightning speed. This training made the folk of the Viking era feared in battle. It was said that the gods themselves wrestled Glima, and the god of Glima was none other than the mighty Thor himself.

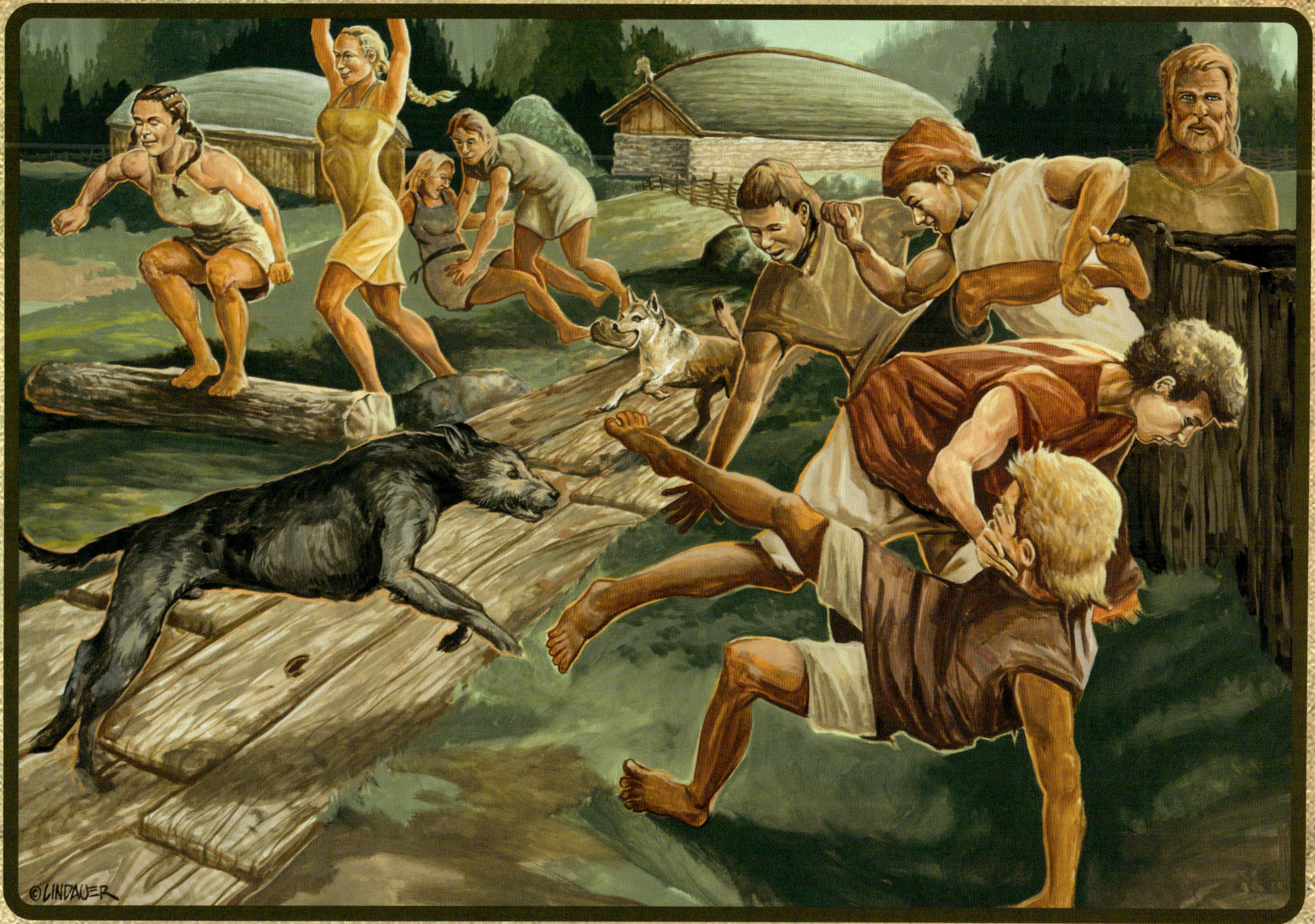
©LINDAUER

In a tangle of limbs, an individual used the strategies they had learned to press the advantage quickly.

Fathers and uncles stood by to coach and referee. While the training was fun, it had to be done correctly for a person to be proficient. Trainers would be sure everyone learned the rules of honor, how to win humbly and lose with grace,

Wrestling and water sports were fun and fitness rolled into one. Games and outdoor activities were great teaching opportunities of important survival skills.

Canines were trained as well to learn the difference between games, a real threat, and when to jump in.....teeth glaring. There are stories of trained "Battle Dogs" in Old Norse culture that were used for family protection, and travel by ship, much like modern-day canine police units.

All original paintings in this book are
available in high-quality
Limited Edition canvas reproductions,
Numbered and Signed by the artist
Only 50 available of each image.
Go to lindauerart.com
for price list , ordering information
and availability

Acknowledgements

Without the following people having been here to help me create this book and all of its content, it would never have come to fruition,
MANY THANKS to
Vivian Kuala, Doug Nordberg, Chris and Teresa Dehart,
Jim Hagstrom, Emily Blair, Randy and Trey Smith,
Katrina Haworth,
Anita Kellerby, Hannah Barefoot,
Tate, Troy, Jennifer, Rae, Lauren, Meg, Frankie Edwards,
Marilyn Bainbridge, the Winzenried family,
Suzanne Rullman, Chan, Bev, Scott and Misty Richard,
Aaron Connelly, Kyle Krietzman, Ross Mickelson,
Sonja, Noelle, Madalyn, Brad Geuke
Bethany Taylor, Jason Winzenried, Taylor Baggs
Kirsten Joy Weiss
Ray "Padre" Johnson , Anette Guldager Boye,
Rich and Christy Tobias, Scott and Stacy Springer,
Corey and Cynthia Sommer, Gordy Stoltz, Jack Anderberg,
John Wickel , Jim Stapleton
Maria Norgaard and Jonas Lau Markussen
Norman and Ramona Lindauer
all Acadamiens uploading thier papers to Academia.edu
And if i have forgotten anyone please forgive..
.you know who you are!
D. Sven Lindauer   Cody, Wyoming 2020